# INVASIVE SPECIES
# ZEBRA MUSSELS

by Alicia Z. Klepeis

pogo

# Ideas for Parents and Teachers

Pogo Books let children practice reading informational text while introducing them to nonfiction features such as headings, labels, sidebars, maps, and diagrams, as well as a table of contents, glossary, and index.

Carefully leveled text with a strong photo match offers early fluent readers the support they need to succeed.

## Before Reading

- "Walk" through the book and point out the various nonfiction features. Ask the student what purpose each feature serves.
- Look at the glossary together. Read and discuss the words.

## Read the Book

- Have the child read the book independently.
- Invite him or her to list questions that arise from reading.

## After Reading

- Discuss the child's questions. Talk about how he or she might find answers to those questions.
- Prompt the child to think more. Ask: Zebra mussels eat a lot. They take food away from native animals. Can you name any other animals that do this?

Pogo Books are published by Jump!
5357 Penn Avenue South
Minneapolis, MN 55419
www.jumplibrary.com

Library of Congress Cataloging-in-Publication Data

Names: Klepeis, Alicia, 1971- author.
Title: Zebra mussels / by Alicia Z. Klepeis.
Description: Minneapolis: Jump!, Inc., [2023]
Series: Invasive species | Includes index.
Audience: Ages 7-10
Identifiers: LCCN 2022006517 (print)
LCCN 2022006518 (ebook)
ISBN 9781636908045 (hardcover)
ISBN 9781636908052 (paperback)
ISBN 9781636908069 (ebook)
Subjects: LCSH: Zebra mussel–Juvenile literature. Invasive species–Juvenile literature.
Classification: LCC QL430.7.D8 K54 2023 (print) | LCC QL430.7.D8 (ebook) | DDC 594/.4–dc23/eng/20220228
LC record available at https://lccn.loc.gov/2022006517
LC ebook record available at https://lccn.loc.gov/2022006518

Editor: Eliza Leahy
Designer: Michelle Sonnek

Photo Credits: 1082492116/Shutterstock, cover; blickwinkel/Alamy, 1, 10-11; Hans Leijnse/Minden Pictures/SuperStock, 3; RLS Photo/Shutterstock, 4; Sam Stukel/South Dakota Game, Fish and Parks, 5; Dragos Asaftei/Shutterstock, 6-7; undefined undefined/iStock, 8; SAPhotog/Shutterstock, 9; Steven Heim/Shutterstock, 12-13; Luke Durda/Alamy, 14-15 (top); Natural History Collection/Alamy, 14-15 (bottom); Michael Schnetzer/USACE Omaha District, 16-17; Anthony Souffle/TNS/Newscom, 18; David Brewster/Star Tribune/Getty, 19; aceshot1/Shutterstock, 20-21; Vitalii Hulai/Shutterstock, 23.

Printed in the United States of America at Corporate Graphics in North Mankato, Minnesota.

# TABLE OF CONTENTS

# CHAPTER 1

# STRIPED SHELLS

What **mollusk** has stripes like a zebra's? It is a zebra **mussel**! Its shell is hard. Inside, its body is soft.

shell

Zebra mussels can be up to two inches (5.1 centimeters) long. But many are smaller than a penny!

Black Sea

Danube River

Zebra mussels live in fresh water. They are mostly found in rivers, streams, lakes, and ponds. They are **native** to eastern Europe and western Asia. In these areas, they live in rivers and lakes connected to seas. The Danube River is one. It connects to the Black Sea.

**DID YOU KNOW?**

Zebra mussels can live in water that has some salt in it. But they cannot live in the ocean. Ocean water is too salty.

# CHAPTER 2

# A STICKY SITUATION

Zebra mussels are an **invasive species** in many areas. How did they get to new places? Their bodies make sticky threads. The threads help them stick to ships, **buoys**, and docks. When a ship moves to a new area, so does the zebra mussel!

threads

They also travel in the **ballast water** of ships. This is probably how they got to North America. They were first found in the Great Lakes area in the late 1980s. Within 10 years, they spread to the Mississippi, Tennessee, and Ohio Rivers.

ballast water

How have they spread so fast? One adult female can produce 1 million eggs each year! **Larvae** hatch. They grow shells within a few days. They swim and eat. A few weeks pass. They attach to something underwater. They usually stay there for life.

# TAKE A LOOK!

Where do zebra mussels live in North America? Take a look!

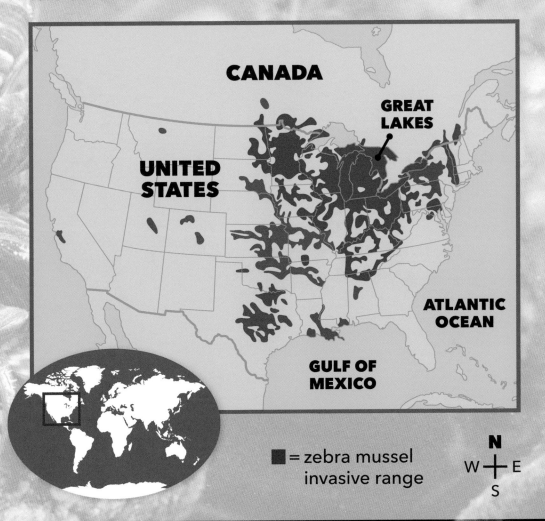

CANADA

GREAT
LAKES

UNITED
STATES

ATLANTIC
OCEAN

GULF OF
MEXICO

■ = zebra mussel
invasive range

N
W ─┼─ E
S

Zebra mussels have few **predators**. This helps their numbers grow. Birds such as herring gulls and diving ducks eat them. But most fish cannot. Why? They can't crush the mussels' shells.

## DID YOU KNOW?

Zebra mussels don't have eyes. They can't see. But they can **sense** things nearby. They close their shells if they are bothered.

shad

fatmuckets

Zebra mussels eat a lot. They mainly eat **plankton**. This takes food away from native animals, like shad and fatmuckets.

**DID YOU KNOW?**

Zebra mussels often kill native mussels. How? They attach to their shells. The native mussels can't move or eat.

Zebra mussels cause problems for humans, too. They often **clog** water pipes. We need the pipes for tap water. Power plants use them, too. It costs millions of dollars to remove the mussels each year.

## DID YOU KNOW?

Zebra mussels often live close together. Nearly 200,000 could fit on top of a school desk!

clogged
pipe

# CHAPTER 3

# MOVE OUT, MUSSELS!

Scientists study zebra mussels. They **track** them. This helps scientists learn where they could spread next.

zebra mussels

People who use boats can help. How? They can clean mussels off the boats and docks they use. This reduces the chance of the mussels spreading to new areas.

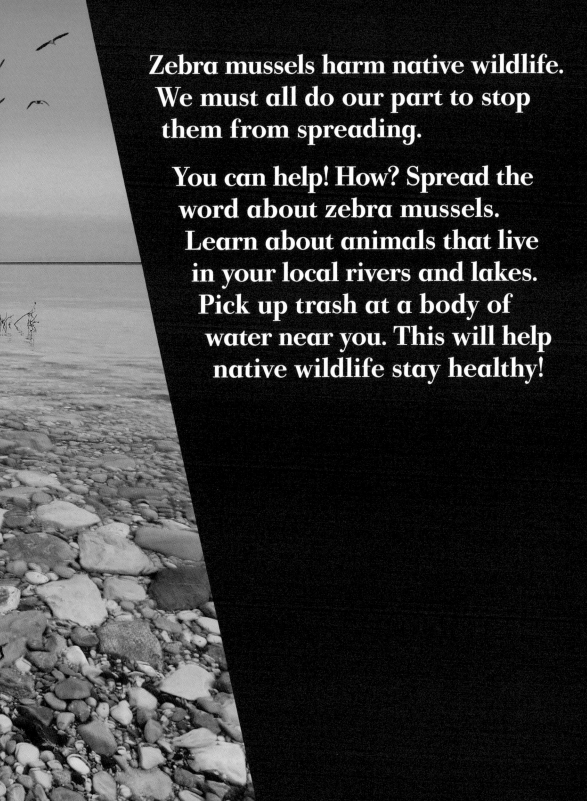

Zebra mussels harm native wildlife. We must all do our part to stop them from spreading.

You can help! How? Spread the word about zebra mussels. Learn about animals that live in your local rivers and lakes. Pick up trash at a body of water near you. This will help native wildlife stay healthy!

# ACTIVITIES & TOOLS

### ZEBRA MUSSEL MATH

Zebra mussels often live in big clusters. Use math to figure out how many could fit in certain areas in this activity!

**What You Need:**
- measuring tape
- masking tape
- computer or calculator
- sheet of paper or notebook
- pencil or pen

1 Use a measuring tape to measure a square on the floor that is three feet (0.9 meters) long by three feet (0.9 m) wide. Mark the square with masking tape. More than 700,000 zebra mussels could fit in this area!

2 Use the measuring tape and masking tape to mark an area that is half the size of the square in Step 1. Use your computer or calculator to find out how many zebra mussels could fit in this area. Write down the answer.

3 Use the measuring tape and masking tape to mark an area that is twice the size of the square in Step 1. How many zebra mussels could fit in this area? Record your answer.

4 How do you think the numbers you recorded compare to the number of zebra mussels in an entire lake or river?

# GLOSSARY

**ballast water:** Water that is held in tanks and cargo holds of ships to keep the ships stable.

**buoys:** Floating markers that warn boats of underwater dangers or show them where to go.

**clog:** To fill up or block something.

**invasive species:** Any kind of living organism that is not native to a specific area.

**larvae:** Young mussels that have recently hatched from eggs.

**mollusk:** An animal with a soft body and a hard shell that lives in water or a damp habitat.

**mussel:** A type of shellfish that has a long, dark shell.

**native:** Growing or living naturally in a particular area of the world.

**plankton:** Tiny animals and plants that drift or float in oceans and lakes.

**predators:** Animals that hunt other animals for food.

**sense:** To feel or become aware of something.

**track:** To follow and try to find an animal by looking for marks or traces of it.

## INDEX

## TO LEARN MORE

Finding more information is as easy as 1, 2, 3.

❶ Go to www.factsurfer.com

❷ Enter "zebramussels" into the search box.

❸ Choose your book to see a list of websites.

FACT
SURFER